Hot Potato
and
Cold Potato

By Graham Meadows

This is a hot potato,
and this is a cold potato.

This is a black dog,
and this is a white dog.

This is a happy clown,
and this is a sad clown.

This is a big elephant,
and this is a little elephant.

This is a fast boat,
and this is a slow boat.

This is a soft candy,
and this is a hard candy.

This is a full bathtub,
and this is an empty bathtub.